LEADERSHIP PRESENCE

How to Show Up, Stand Out, & Shake Up the World

D1561962

If no one tells you they believe in you,
I believe in you.

LEADERSHIP PRESENCE
by Justin Patton

Printed in the United States of America.
SECOND EDITION. July 2020.

LEADERSHIP PRESENCE
How to Show Up, Stand Out, & Shake Up the World

ISBN 978-1-7328766-6-8 (paperback)
ISBN 978-1-7328766-4-4 (ebook)

Written by Justin Patton
Designed by Shaina Nielson

DEDICATION

This book was written for you because of your desire to shake up the world and stand out for all the right reasons!

TABLE OF CONTENTS

The not-so-subtle case
for gentleness...1

Competition and
leadership presence..9

The fundamentals of
leadership presence...13

Debunking 5 myths about
leadership presence...23

The #1 trait that will erode
leadership presence, instantly..................................37

11 actionable tips to maximize
your leadership presence......................................41

10 questions to ask yourself
about leadership presence.....................................72

Final thoughts..74

THE
NOT-SO-SUBTLE
CASE FOR
GENTLENESS

"

In a gentle way,
you can
shake up the world.

–Gandhi

"

You have the power, right now, to use your presence to make an incredible difference in how other people think and act. Your ability to shake up the world and challenge individuals to see themselves and others differently makes you a leader.

But how you shake up the world makes all the difference. Some people do it through fear and aggression. Others shake up the world through kindness and gentle assertiveness. Both methods work, but gentleness will always outlast aggression. More importantly, how you shake up the world says a lot about your character.

You probably know a leader who has made it to the top of an organization or who is renowned in their industry, but who was a bully and rewarded for bad behavior. Outward success does not equate with leadership presence or a positive legacy.

There have been plenty of leaders in history who achieved outward success at the costs of other people. It might make for good television like Miranda Priestly in *The Devil Wears Prada or Dave Harken in Horrible Bosses 2*, but that behavior in the real world only serves to create a toxic culture that erodes trust.

Look at individuals who sabotaged careers because of their repeated pattern of bad behavior: former Uber CEO Travis Kalanick; former head of retail banking for Wells Fargo, Carrie Tolstedt; NASCAR driver Kurt Busch; and former Indiana basketball coach Bobby Knight.

Why are these types of leaders often allowed to get away with this behavior for so long?

It's because many of these individuals are high performers who get results. Most organizations don't address bad behavior with an individual until specific actions become problematic for their direct supervisor or the company's reputation. Only then does it get addressed immediately.

Company culture is based on the behavior rewarded. When an organization only rewards results, and not how people get results, they create a toxic culture that permeates every level in the organization. They always wake up years later wondering how they got here and how to change the culture.

The quickest way to create a culture change in any organization is by rewarding leadership presence, and that is why the case for gentleness is necessary.

Gentleness is the essence of leadership presence, and the only way to earn and keep trust.

Gentleness is defined as the quality of being kind or mild-mannered. At its core, gentleness is about being a good human being, and I believe we can all agree we need more of that in the world.

Gentleness isn't weakness, nor is it acquiescing to the whims of others. Gentleness is about acting and responding in ways that demonstrate the best of who you are.

Gentleness requires healthy emotional intelligence. It means being unafraid to show up and stand out. It is, however, a deliberate focus on *how*. Some of the best leaders in history, and some of the most recognized leaders today, demonstrate that you can stand up for what you believe, disrupt the status quo, and do it without sacrificing your character. A few of those gentle giants who are known for their positive results and approaches include Martin Luther King, Jr., Mother Teresa, Colin Kaepernick, Pat Summitt, Greg Creed (former CEO of Yum! Brands), Lynsi Synder (CEO of In-N-Out Burger), and Jeff Weiner (CEO of LinkedIn).

I've found, in more than a decade of leadership and coaching experience, that competence never held any of my clients back. Each problem they faced came down to relationships and how their actions eroded trust. It was their lack of gentleness that ultimately held them back.

I coached an executive leader at a Fortune 500 company who was one of the brightest people I ever met. His problem, however, was his constant need to prove his intelligence. He was always the first to speak in meetings. He played Devil's Advocate to everyone else's ideas. He was quick to become defensive. Most of his actions were driven by fear and the need to garner compliance. As a result, he eroded trust among many of his peers.

My job as his coach was to help him explore other ways of leading and communicating. The way he showed up was transactional. We discovered his transactional approach in the office was similar to his approach with his wife and kids.

He wanted healthier relationships. He just didn't have the awareness and skillset he needed, in that moment, to show up and stand out in a way that built trust.

It took months of coaching, but he slowly started to see the rewards of leading and communicating in a more gentle way. Leading gently did not require him to change who he was. It required that he slow down, discover who he was authentically, and live in that space more often.

Getting results and making it to the top levels of an organization does not have to be a lonely place, but it will be when you've ruined relationships on your way to the top.

There may be some of you who cannot get on board with the idea of gentleness because of how you've chosen to interpret that word. I honor where you are in your journey.

I would invite you, however, to look at your current relationships and identify how your presence is impacting trust. If trust is not where you want it to be, you might ask that individual, "What can I do to build more trust with you in our relationship?" Stay curious about what they have to say. I asked my best friend this question. He replied, "Get my name tattooed on your chest." Use your best judgment when taking advice from those friends. My hope is that when you're ready to do this type of work, my book will serve as your starting point.

Gentleness does not ask you to compromise who you are. If anything, it invites you to find even more powerful ways to lead, love, and communicate with trust. For those of you ready to embrace gentleness as your strength, let's get started.

The best leaders, who leave a positive legacy people never forget, have one thing in common: *leadership presence.*

COMPETITION AND LEADERSHIP PRESENCE

Pat Summit is one of the most successful basketball coaches of all time and a leader I admire. She used to tell her players, "Life is competitive. People are going to keep score, and it does matter. You cannot be afraid to go out and compete."

I love competition! In fact, one of my personal mottos is, "Sometimes you win. Sometimes you win more." Competition challenges us to grow and it pushes us further than we ever thought possible. My earliest memories of competing are from Boy Scouts. That foundation instilled the belief that it's okay to compete with integrity and show others what you've learned. Winning a gold medal in the world championships with The Cavaliers Drum and Bugle Corps taught me that the road to victory is paved with lots of small failures and wins. They are all necessary to compete at the highest levels. Winning feels good because it is recognition of your hard work, but how you win is what ultimately shapes your legacy.

Jesse Owens has been noted in history for competing with dignity and grace. He competed in front of Adolf Hitler during the 1936 Olympics in Berlin. Owens, under immense pressure, fouled out on his first two qualifying long jumps.

His main rival, German Luz Long, came over and introduced himself. He suggested that Jesse move his take-off mark back and play it safe. This would allow Owens to qualify easily. Owens took his competitor's advice and successfully qualified for the finals where he went on to win the gold medal. Luz Long won silver, and he was the first person to congratulate Owens. They embraced in front of Hitler, and their friendship was cemented.

Owens later wrote, "You can melt down all the medals and cups I have, and they wouldn't be a plating on the 24-karat friendship I felt for Luz Long at that moment."

These world-class athletes prove that you can be a gentle competitor. You can be kind and look out for others while relentlessly pursuing your dreams, too.

This concept applies just as much to business as to sports. A whiskey distillery in Kentucky found out the grain they received from a supplier didn't meet their quality standards. The leadership team immediately stopped production at the plant and contacted their competitors to let them know about the grain issue. Yes, this distributor wants to be the best. They are going to compete in the marketplace and try to out-sell their competition. However, they recognize they can be a good sport and look out for others in the process.

Both examples above demonstrate the art of leadership presence.

Never be fooled into believing you have to choose between winning and gentleness. The best leaders do both.

THE
FUNDAMENTALS
OF LEADERSHIP
PRESENCE

I boarded a Delta flight from Tampa to Atlanta on December 13, 2018. I found my seat, put my headphones in, and prepared to block out the world for the remainder of the trip. A mom then boarded the plane with her teenage son, who was disabled. He was carried onto the flight by airline staff and buckled into his seat. During the boarding process, the boy was mumbling and yelling throughout the cabin because he could not communicate with words. I paused my headphones and watched the beautiful way this mother interacted with her son. She remained calm throughout the flight, demonstrated patience, and was there for her son every step of the way. Her presence made an impact on me that day that I've remembered for years.

Another travel incident didn't leave me with the same feeling. It was a long travel day, but I finally arrived in Dallas at 11:30 pm. I made it to the National Rental Car counter where there was a line of people waiting for cars. One by one, we waited as the staff instructed us when to head outside and claim a vehicle. A gentleman and I were sent out at the same time since there were three available cars. He went to one that had flashing lights, and I went to one that had the trunk up. I was confused if someone had already claimed the car since the trunk was up. I looked at him and said I wasn't sure what was going on.

He walked over, put his luggage in the trunk, and said, "Well, I'll take this one. I was ahead of you, anyway." I was so shocked at his behavior that I just stood there thinking about whether I would let it go or go to jail. By the time I made a rational choice, he was already in the car driving away. It made me curious if he was having a bad day or if that is how he treats everyone in life. Regardless, I will never forget the feeling he left on me that day.

Presence is the style you show up with and how that style makes other people feel.

Those undeniable feelings last long after you're gone. Those feelings are based on their perceptions, and those perceptions impact the quality of your relationships.

Your presence is either opening or closing doors for you. The more aware you are about the difference your presence makes in your life and the lives of others, the better prepared you'll be to compete at the top of your game.

We all have presence, but not everyone has leadership presence.

Leadership presence is using your style to earn others' confidence and trust. It's the way we expect and need leaders to show up if we are to put our trust in them. Leadership presence is always a result of a people-first mindset. That mindset influences your style, and your style dictates what you believe about yourself and how you communicate.

Leadership presence has nothing to do with titles, age, or seniority. It has everything to do with self-awareness, authenticity, and the desire to want to connect deeply with others. The best leaders are those who make others better and leave a positive legacy we never forget.

New York Governor Andrew Cuomo was widely recognized and applauded for his response to the coronavirus pandemic. He managed to show up and stand out in a way that built high levels of trust with his constituents. He did this by first providing daily televised briefings where he was scrupulous with the truth. Second, he was transparent about why his administration made the decisions they made. His transparency created clarity and certainty. Third, he communicated with tact. His approach was one of both confidence and humility. He pushed back when necessary but never let his intensity overshadow the message. He demonstrated deep empathy for front-line responders and for the people who lost their lives to the virus. Finally, his messages were always focused on a theme of togetherness and doing what was best for the community as a whole. His presence has become a model on how we expect leaders to lead in crisis.

Leadership presence is a win-win for everyone. It's not a tactic used to manipulate or get what you want. At your worst, your presence is self-serving and fosters disconnection. At your best, your presence makes people feel more connected and less alone in the world. That's when the people you're communicating with feel safe and connected. It's only then that they are in a place to hear your message.

I've always believed that your leadership presence becomes a differentiator that organizations want to invest in, where people are eager to build genuine relationships with you, and where you become a trusted voice.

WHAT THE RESEARCH SAYS

According to research from the Center for Talent Innovation, in a survey of 268 senior executives, leadership presence is based on three foundational factors:

- How you look (appearance – 5%)
- How you speak (communication – 28%)
- How you act (gravitas – 67%)

All three factors impact your ability to have leadership presence. Below is a summary of these three factors I highlighted in my previous book about leadership, *Bold New You*.

HOW YOU LOOK

Your appearance matters. It might make up only five percent of your overall leadership presence, but that number packs a big punch! Image is the first credibility hurdle you must pass professionally. People should not be so distracted by your appearance that they can't hear your message. If this happens, you damage your credibility.

You should always tailor your appearance to the culture of an organization. The culture of the organization impacts how others view your presence. It is a signal that "this person gets who we are." For example, I wear nice jeans and a dress shirt when I speak at Taco Bell's Restaurant Support Center. I wear more-formal business attire when I work with chambers of commerce across the United States. Leadership presence doesn't ask you to compromise who you are. You can be authentic and have a signature style while still fitting into the organizational culture.

HOW YOU SPEAK

Communication comprises 28% of your executive presence. How you speak is just as important, if not more important, than what you speak about.

We live in a world where we're always communicating—whether through words, body language, or digital footprint. Authenticity requires you to communicate your brand in a way that aligns to your values. That means there should be no difference in how you communicate personally or professionally. Your values are not situational.

HOW YOU ACT

Gravitas is the seriousness and weight of your demeanor, and it constitutes 67% of your leadership presence. In short, gravitas means your sincerity and dignity. We all know leaders who are smart but lack awareness about how their intensity may impact others in the room. It is their lack of gravitas that will prevent them from reaching their leadership potential.

Gravitas is similar to the word gravity. Gravity keeps us grounded, and it connects us with the center of the Earth. Gravitas keeps us grounded in our emotional intelligence and connected with our higher self at all times, but especially during stressful times when things don't go as planned.

The main characteristics of gravitas, as identified by leaders in the Center for Talent Innovation's leadership survey, were *confidence* and *grace under fire*. These are the most important traits to show people that you have good leadership presence.

PUTTING IT ALL TOGETHER

At its core, leadership presence is all about trust. Trustworthiness is your most important competitive advantage. You will never earn trust through fear and aggression. That's a short-term strategy to force compliance out of people. Instead, you earn and keep people's trust through consistent gentleness. This is the only strategy that allows leaders to create long-term commitments.

Each day offers you the chance to show up with leadership presence in your relationships, in the workplace, in public, in how you compete, and of course in parenting. You won't always get it right. Be gentle with yourself. That road to victory is paved with lots of failures and lessons to help you grow.

You have everything you need to show up and stand out. I want you to go out and compete in life. I want you to be the go-to choice when people need someone. More importantly, I want you to believe in yourself so wholeheartedly that you realize your presence can change the world – gently, purposefully, and through trust.

DEBUNKING 5 MYTHS ABOUT LEADERSHIP PRESENCE

MYTH #1:
All leaders have leadership presence

All leaders have presence, but not all leaders have leadership presence.

Presence is simply the feeling you leave on people. Based on that feeling, people make instant judgments which influence their level of trust in you.

Years ago, I was standing in line at a popular Mexican restaurant where you order your food and they make it right there in front of you. I ordered a chicken quesadilla and asked for it to be cooked twice. I waited patiently for the timer to go off. After the second time, the young lady making my food hit the button for the third time. I politely leaned forward and said, "Excuse me. I only need it cooked twice." She cranked her head around slowly, looked straight at me, lifted her eyebrows, and said, "I KNOW!" She then plopped my quesadilla on the counter, slid it toward me, and walked off as if on an episode of America's Next Top Model. Her presence was so dismissive that I immediately tweeted their corporate headquarters, told everyone I could about the experience, and never went back.

This example demonstrates the incredible power of our presence. Presence can disrupt thinking, impact decision making, inspire loyalty or drive change. When we use our presence for good, we move from just presence to leadership presence.

Leadership presence is using your style to earn others' confidence and trust.

Oprah Winfrey has built a fortune of more than two billion dollars from her hard work and business acumen; but more importantly, from her ability to connect with others. She has used her presence as a "force for good" and earned massive amounts of trust and confidence from people as a result. Once people buy into her as a trustful, compassionate person, they also buy into the topics she shares, the products she sells, and the movement she creates. Her leadership presence is an undeniable reason for her success, and it can be for yours as well.

MYTH #2:
A great way to build presence is to "fake it until you make it"

People often have good intentions when they tell someone to "fake it until you make it," but it's awful advice, and we need to stop saying it.

First, leadership presence is built on the premise of authenticity and connection, not a one-size-fits-all approach. Therefore, anyone who already knew how to show up and "make it," would have done so. Consequently, they have a limited understanding of what "fake it until you make it" actually means, so they try to fill in the rest of the meaning with their narrow understanding or through advice and ideas from others. As a result, these individuals typically over-compensate and let their intensity get in the way of success.

Second, people who fake-it-to-make-it generally show up in a conversation eager to apply a bunch of tactics they've learned. These tactics may work, but when the scenario doesn't go as planned, the individual often becomes rigid and lacks enough flexibility to go where the conversation organically leads them. As a result, they often revert to their old ways.

Third, it perpetuates the idea that you should "own the room." **Leadership presence is about owning your energy and style, not the room.** When you walk into a room with the intention to "own it," you step into your ego and make the moment all about yourself and your needs.

Owning your energy and style means you align your appearance, your words, and your actions to build trust and connection in that situation. It doesn't require you to shrink or be any less vocal with your contributions. It does, however, require you to focus on how you show up and if you're doing so in a way that builds relationships.

Instead of telling someone to "fake it until you make it," it's better to help them understand who they are when they're at their best, and give them enough awareness and tools to stay in that space.

Only when you stop faking it can you actually make it.

MYTH #3:
You are either born with leadership presence or you're not

Leadership presence is not an innate characteristic. Instead, leadership presence is learned through role modeling, deepening your level of emotional intelligence, being open to feedback, and through intentional practice.

Role Modeling
Some of our best learning moments come from watching others and using them as role models on what to do.

I've always admired the leadership presence of former Secretary of State Condoleezza Rice. She speaks with quiet confidence. She articulates a clear point of view, and she's not afraid to push back with grace and tact.

I've also watched leaders and learned what not to do. We can learn from both types of leaders. Here are three questions you should ask yourself to learn from role models:

1. What is the feeling or impression that person leaves on people?
2. What did they do to give me that feeling?
3. What will I do differently as a result of what I experienced?

Emotional Intelligence

Emotional intelligence is the ability to use emotions in a way that builds trust and moves relationships forward.

This requires self-awareness of presence as well as managing that presence. As a result, you can build mutually beneficial relationships with others.

The core emotional intelligence traits which I teach are confidence, empathy, impulse control, emotional expression, and optimism. These are the ones I believe significantly impact leadership presence.

When we show up demonstrating those traits in healthy ways, we can always connect better with ourselves and with others.

All emotions serve a purpose, and we get to decide how to use those emotions. The more focused you are on growing your emotional intelligence, the stronger your leadership presence will be.

Be Open to Feedback

I had a boss who said, "All feedback is information. You get to decide what you do with that information."

Leadership presence is all about creating trust and showing up your best. You're not always going to get it right. Therefore, you need feedback – especially from the people that have your best interest in mind.

One piece of feedback that changed my life came to me while hiking in Italy with two friends. They said, "We feel that we often get all of you or none of you, and we think the best version of you is somewhere in the middle." They were right.

I've spent years learning to balance my approach and not let my intensity underwhelm or overwhelm how I show up with others. I don't always get it right, but this feedback has made me more intentional, and I get it right more often than I get it wrong. This is why we need feedback in our lives.

Intentional Practice

Developing your leadership presence is not about changing you. It's about reminding yourself of who you are when you're at your best, and consistently showing up that way. This takes intentional practice.

I once coached a client whose goal was to learn how to be in relationships without exhausting people. He acknowledged that his approach – both personally and professionally – was very transactional. He often got what he wanted at the moment, but his relationships always suffered in the long-term. He came to understand that if he were going to truly improve, then he must genuinely want his relationships to last longer than the task. With that awareness, he could start to make different choices that built trust and confidence in his relationships. It was the intentional daily practice that helped him turn his relationships around.

Here is an exercise you can do to figure out who you are at your best:

1. Recall a specific time when you showed up at your best.
2. What were the top 3 qualities you demonstrated at that moment?
3. How did you feel showing up like that?
4. Finish this line "At my best, I am . . . " (List your top 3 consistent qualities.)

That's the truth about who you are! Now your job is to ensure your choices align with that truth, and practice it daily.

MYTH #4:
Leadership presence is all about projecting strength

Confidence is a prerequisite for leadership presence. Yet, it would be misguided to believe that the only way to demonstrate confidence is by projecting strength.

My pastor once said, "You cannot meet people where they are when you think you're above them." There's a time to be confident and powerful, but there's also a time to be empathetic and collaborative. Leadership presence requires you to have an awareness about how to flex your communication style and meet people where they are. We aren't one-dimensional beings who only show up with one way of communicating. Flexibility in our approach is the hallmark of healthy emotional intelligence and our desire to connect.

From the perspective of body language, confidence is conveyed by taking up space, making yourself naturally bigger, and asserting a point of view when you can move the conversation forward. For example, it would be appropriate to show up with confidence when you're proposing your ideas in a meeting, or giving a speech.

However, the body language of empathy and collaboration looks completely different. It doesn't require taking up a lot of space or making yourself bigger. Instead, the body language of empathy invites you to make yourself smaller sometimes, so you can make an audience feel more comfortable and safe. Examples of situations when it might be appropriate to use the body language of empathy include times when you're listening deeply or having a difficult conversation.

Great leaders know how to flex their style and meet people where they are.

Sometimes people experience your confidence through strength and assertiveness. Sometimes they experience your confidence through empathy and deep listening.

The best leaders, with the best leadership presence, can flex their style within the same conversation to focus on trust and connection.

MYTH #5:
Leadership presence requires you to know the answers

While having answers and demonstrating a strong knowledge base in your area of expertise are essential for credibility, leadership presence doesn't require you to know all the answers or never make mistakes.

James Kouzes and Barry Posner are leading researchers on leadership credibility. Their survey on "Characteristics of Admired Leaders" has been completed by over seventy-five thousand people around the world. The top trait, and the one with the most impact on the relationship with others, has consistently been *honesty*. Competence has ranked between second and fourth on the list over the years. This proves that "smarts" are important, but they aren't everything.

Leadership presence requires you to be transparent with people when you don't know the answer, or when you get it wrong. It means having enough confidence to let people know you'll find out the answer, or you'll do everything possible to make the situation right.

It takes humility to acknowledge when you don't have all the answers, and the door to authentic confidence and connection is through humility.

The word "humility" comes from the Latin word *humilis*, which means "low." We can interpret that to mean grounded, not putting yourself below or above other people. Humility builds our authentic confidence because it forces us to be real about who we are and what we desire. It requires that we give up any sense of entitlement we think we're owed, and believe that we're not higher or lower than each other.

Humility takes powerful inner strength because it challenges us to take the spotlight off ourselves and. . .

- Get comfortable talking about our shortcomings
- Allow others the same space to share their perspectives
- Care about the needs of others
- Recognize others for their contributions
- Acknowledge our missteps
- Apologize when it's warranted

It's unrealistic to have all the answers. Release yourself from that burden. Great leaders aren't worried about being the smartest person in the room. Instead, they're focused on surrounding themselves with the right people who can help them get the information and communicate honestly with the people they serve.

THE #1 TRAIT THAT WILL ERODE YOUR LEADERSHIP PRESENCE, INSTANTLY

The #1 trait that will erode your leadership presence instantly is ego.

Ego is any fear-based thought that pulls you out of alignment with the truth of who you are.

Fear-based thoughts drive your inner critic, influence your posturing, thwart your self-awareness, and erode your leadership presence.

The most damaging consequence of ego is that it fosters disconnection. If you become detached from the truth of who you are, you may act in ways that are beneath you. As a result, you lose the trust and confidence of others. All relationships suffer when you lean into your ego more than you lean into your inner truth.

Your ego always catapults you to an extreme version of yourself. When this happens, your mindset and actions show up in one of two ways: *bravado* or *self-doubt*.

Individuals who respond from a place of bravado mask their fear with aggression and armor. They go out to face the world with this over-the-top façade of confidence.

Others respond to their fear by surrendering every ounce of personal power. Their posturing comes across as self-doubt, and instead of living their lives as champions for themselves and others, they become victims.

The longer you reside in either one of these extreme spaces, the more comfortable you become. The more comfortable you are, the more you'll believe it's your authentic self. Don't be fooled: **the best version of you never operates in extreme places.**

You'll know you're operating from your ego the moment you. . .

- Make everything about you
- Become critical and judgmental
- Listen with the intent to be right
- Allow your intensity to hold you back
- Believe your truth is the only truth
- Ignore feedback and coaching
- Take no accountability for your actions

We all have ego. Ego itself is not the problem. It is one's lack of awareness about their ego that is the problem.

Once you realize that you're starting to operate from ego, you can begin to make different choices. The best strategy I can suggest is to stay curious. We show up differently when coming from a place of curiosity. When we sit back and resist the desire to be right or critical, we become more open-minded and see things we wouldn't have seen before.

Leadership presence means you have enough awareness to know when you are operating from your ego, and the self-management to make different choices to help you earn others' trust and confidence.

11 ACTIONABLE TIPS TO MAXIMIZE YOUR LEADERSHIP PRESENCE

Most people that you meet will never know you at the level of your family or friends. Most people will only catch glimpses of you, and they will make judgments that impact your life based on those glimpses.

Great leaders manage the glimpses people see, in order to compete at the top of the game and stand out for all the right reasons.

Here are 11 actionable tips to maximize your leadership presence:

1. Master your inner game
2. Learn to see yourself
3. Make your appearance matter
4. Act like you belong
5. Love people enough to tell them the truth
6. Put empathy before information
7. Manage your intensity
8. Play the long game
9. Stop putting your identity on the line
10. Protect your online presence
11. Vent in private, lead in public

TIP #1:
Master your inner game

Leadership presence starts on the inside with your mindset. It's your thinking, whether conscious or unconscious, that drives how you look, how you speak, and how you act.

When we only focus on how people show up outwardly and fail to address mindset, we teach them to play a part instead of being authentic. Leadership presence isn't a performance. It's the authentic alignment between your thoughts and actions.

In my workbook on confidence, *Unleashing Potential*, I say, "There is nothing more important in the world than your belief in yourself. What you believe about yourself becomes the filter for how you show up in the world, how you make decisions, and how you treat yourself and others."

Success always starts with your mindset. I teach people that "Leadership is not about you, but it starts with you." If we genuinely believe in authentic leadership, then we must take the time to help individuals understand their thinking around core values, purpose, emotional triggers, patterns of behavior, and emotional intelligence. All of these factors influence how someone shows up every day, in every part of their life.

There is a lot of research about the connection between our thoughts, feelings, and actions. We know that our thoughts lead to our feelings, which lead to our actions. Here are three examples of how that works in life.

THOUGHTS	FEELINGS	ACTIONS
Oh my gosh. I can't do this!	Anxiety and Embarrassment	You don't try, become defensive
I can't believe he just said that. Really?	Judgmental and Critical	Dismissive of the individual
I haven't felt this way in a long time.	Joy and Excitement	You invest in the relationship

When you understand that thoughts are driving your actions, you can tune in and become more aware of your emotions and motivations. You can make choices that better align with how you want to show up in the world. When we lack this awareness, we become more impulsive and justify our bad behaviors. We try to control everyone and everything except the one thing we have power over—our own mindset.

Your mindset is a choice, but that doesn't mean it's an easy one.

We all show up with a mindset of either abundance or scarcity. Sometimes, depending on the circumstances, we find ourselves teetering back and forth between the two. That's normal, but leadership presence requires you to have awareness about your thoughts and choose abundance because it's the pathway that lets you build trust with yourself and others.

When you show up with a mindset of abundance, you find plenty of opportunities in your present moment. That doesn't mean you're out of touch with reality or don't honor your feelings. Instead, it means you acknowledge what is happening, and you still choose to grow. You accept change, find opportunities to get better, share openly with others, and work toward a better future for everyone.

When you show up with a scarcity mindset, your actions are all driven by fear. You're resistant to change, and you become controlling, critical, and overly competitive. You show up with a zero-sum mentality ("for every winner there must be a loser"), so you only look out for yourself. When that happens, trust is always sacrificed.

Your leadership presence is a reflection of your mindset, so always choose one that allows you to build trust and confidence.

Remember: People can only experience you based on what they hear and see on the outside. Yet, what happens inside you determines the quality of their experience. This is why "success is an inside job."

TIP #2:
Learn to see yourself

If I could only share one quote for the rest of my life that I believe has the power to change how we lead, love, and communicate, then it would be one from Oprah. She said...

"Everyone in life just wants to know three things. They want to know: Do you see me? Do you hear me? Does what I say mean anything to you?"

Being seen is one of the greatest gifts we can receive. It makes us feel safe and that who we are matters. It gives us a comfortable space to share our voice, take risks, and lean into our creativity even more. Great leaders always use their presence to make other people feel seen and heard. However, they also know there will be plenty of people who will come in and out of your life that will never make you feel that way. If you wait for their permission and validation, you will wait for a lifetime. Developing leadership presence requires you to focus on the things you can control. **You cannot control whether other people see you, but you can control how you see yourself.**

Michelle Obama, in her 2020 Netflix special *Becoming*, was asked by a young girl, "How do you persevere through invisibility?" She told the girl she never felt invisible because her parents always made her feel seen. She went on to say, "We cannot wait for the world to be equal to start feeling seen…You have to find the tools within yourself to feel visible."

Learning to see yourself is one foundational step to developing authentic confidence, and authentic confidence is the cornerstone of leadership presence. You develop authentic confidence by mastering a deep level of self-awareness and self-acceptance. I shared in my previous book, *Unleashing Potential*, "Authentic confidence from being able to wake up every morning and radically love the person staring back at you in the mirror. Confidence is putting the need to like yourself over the need to be liked by others." This is how you start to see yourself – even when others can't or won't.

One key to seeing yourself is finding and trusting the voice you already have.

In February 2020, Taco Bell hosted an event to recognize and celebrate youth in the Boys and

Girls Club. That is where I had the privilege of meeting Arriyah. Arriyah was a teenager full of life. Her energy was dynamic, her facial expressions hilarious, and her silence made you question what would happen next. She stood confidently in front of 60 restaurant general managers and expressed her desire to be a comedian. We knew by the time she finished speaking she was a star. She used her presence and storytelling, at such a young age, to make people laugh. Her voice transcended age, race, and experiences to connect people through laughter. Afterwards, I asked her if anyone in life ever tells her she is too much and needs to dial it back. She said they did. I could relate. I explained that everything other people think is "too much" about her right now is exactly what will make her successful in the future. I encouraged her to keep sharing her voice because the world needs it more than she even realizes. Before I left, I turned to Arriyah and shared a quote I heard from RuPaul. "You are not too much. You are everything."

I have spoken and coached hundreds of people who want to gain stronger confidence. My best advice on growing confidence is to "find your voice." So many people fool themselves into believing they'll speak up once they're confident.

It doesn't work that way. You will never speak up. You find your voice, and you share it with others – even if you're nervous.

You see yourself every time you believe and trust that someone in that room needs to hear your thoughts, ideas, story in only the way you can say it. This is how you show self-respect to your thoughts and ideas. Most of the time, it will go great. Occasionally, you will wish it went better. It takes all of these experiences to learn and grow. If you want to see yourself, then find and trust the voice you already have.

TIP #3:
Make your appearance matter

How you dress and what your space looks like will be perceived by others as the value you place on yourself. Yes, there is so much more to you than your appearance, but it's the first signal you give others regarding your authenticity and credibility.

Appearance is one of the first credibility hurdles you must pass professionally. According to the Center for Talent Innovation, it constitutes 5% of your overall leadership presence. Still, it's a primary factor by which people decide if they trust you and are open to hearing what you want to say.

People shouldn't be so distracted by your image that they can't hear your message.

I once had a brainstorming session with more than 40 leaders who run multi-million-dollar sales businesses. I asked them their opinions about "appearance derailers" and best practices. Here's what they shared:

Appearance Derailers:

- Clothing too baggy, tight, or wrinkled
- Lacking proper hygiene
- Clothes/Shoes you would wear to the club

Appearance Best Practices:

- Dress to fit the culture of the organization
- Wear clothes tailored to your body type
- Be well-groomed
- Add your own authentic style

Looking good is a matter of perspective, and it's hard to be objective about ourselves. Ask for feedback. Don't let your appearance take away from your intellect. You're meant to stand out, but you'll have a credibility issue if people are talking more about your appearance than your ideas.

TIP #4:
Act like you belong

The most impactful leadership advice I ever heard was from Greg Creed, the former CEO of Yum! Brands. He said, "Stop trying to prove you belong and act like you belong."

I remember being in church one day and a lady in the congregation asked me, "What do you do?" I shared with her that I travel around the country coaching leaders on how to maximize their leadership presence. She responded with admiration and then followed it up by saying, "You seem young." I went on to list my credentials and halfway through my diatribe I thought, *Why are you telling her all this information?* I quickly finished the conversation, but I left there feeling like I had tried to prove myself to her. People who act like they belong don't feel the need to prove themselves to others. They already believe they're good enough.

Acting like you belong is showing up and having confidence in the value your experience and perspective add to the conversation. Whenever you try to prove yourself to others, you step out of your authenticity and damage your credibility. It often comes across as desperate and inauthentic.

The Atlantic published an article in 2014 called "The Confidence Gap." One of the main questions they posed was, "Is confidence just as important as competence?"

The answer is **yes**. "Success, it turns out, correlates just as closely with confidence as it does with competence." The more confident leaders appear, the more competent people perceive them as.

For example, I went to a highly reputable dermatologist in my area to have a cyst removed off the top of my head. As the doctor took the scalpel and cut into my head the nurse gasped and said, "Oh no!" I immediately became anxious and said, "What do you mean 'oh no'?" She said, "It's just bleeding more than I thought it would." I told her, "I'm going to need you to keep that to yourself." These individuals were highly competent in their field, but her words made me doubt her competence. As a patient, I needed her to show up with more authentic confidence in that vulnerable moment.

Acting like you belong does not mean you're "faking it." It's showing up into a space with quiet confidence and ensuring your actions inspire trust and confidence from others. It comes from an authentic place where you don't feel the need to prove yourself. Your words aren't rushed, your passion isn't distracting, you don't take things personally, and you're comfortable choosing when to be silent.

Anyone can have quiet confidence when things are going well, and everyone is getting along. The true measure of your confidence is when you're under pressure and becoming triggered emotionally. When a crisis happens, you want to be a leader who remains calm and emotionally present, and whose energy brings out the best in everyone around you. That's a leader whose presence makes you feel safe, and whom you trust to see you through the difficulties.

TIP #5:
Love people enough to tell them the truth

One of the bravest decisions you will make is to tell someone the truth – even when telling the truth isn't easy or comfortable.

Leadership presence is all about trust; therefore, it requires you to be a defender of truth, and be tactful in how you deliver that truth.

Every time I engage in a difficult conversation, own up to a mistake I've made, give constructive feedback to an employee, or speak in front of a large audience, I remind myself to **"love people enough to tell them the truth."**

This mantra serves as my constant reminder of how to show up in relationships. When we love people enough to tell them the whole truth, then we're transparent. Transparency is an essential factor in earning and keeping trust with others.

Leadership presence mandates that you not only tell your own truth, but you stay curious and open to hearing the other person's truth as well.

I have learned that everyone can handle the truth. What they can't handle are silence and secrecy. Silence and secrecy make trust unrepairable.

In a 2013 article titled *Connect, Then Lead,* Harvard Business Review asked the question, "Is it better to be loved or feared?" The research proved that both fear (defined as strength, agency, or competence) and love (defined as warmth, communion, and trustworthiness) are important, but love needs to come before strength. Researchers emphasized, "Leaders who project strength before establishing trust run the risk of eliciting fear, and along with it a host of dysfunctional behaviors."

You're making every decision either out of love or fear. Truth is always an outgrowth of love, so love yourself and others enough to tell the truth.

TIP # 6:
Put empathy before information

A company I work with had just hired a new president for its business. She had a great energy that matched the culture, but she came from a different industry background, so some employees weren't sure what to expect.

As an effort to build relationships with others, she hosted a meeting where she talked about who she was and allowed them the opportunity to ask questions. A prominent and vocal leader in the room raised his hand and asked, "Why should I trust you?"

It would have been easy at this moment to become defensive or feel the need to prove herself by focusing on her past results. However, the president had enough confidence not to take the comment personally, and the emotional intelligence to answer in a way that made a connection with everyone in the room.

She led her response with empathy and explained that he had every reason not to trust her right now. She then humbly asked him to trust the people who hired her since he believed in them and give her the chance to earn his trust.

She proved that great leaders, especially in moments of emotionally charged situations, put empathy first and information second. It was empathy that allowed her to dampen the intensity in the room while also building her credibility.

I define empathy as the willingness to see beyond yourself. It's the most effective way to build trust when communicating.

Always use empathy when someone is communicating with a lot of emotion. That's a signal they want to be acknowledged for what they're experiencing. Empathy is the key to making people feel heard and understood. It's the fastest way to help them work through their emotions.

TIP #7:
Manage your intensity

Many leaders whom I coach confuse expressing emotion with being emotional.

Understanding and expressing emotion is critical for having healthy relationships and good situational awareness. However, you become emotional when you're triggered by your emotions, and your presence is no longer safe for people to open up and tell the truth.

Emotional behavior always comes across as intensity. Intensity is a turn-off, and it immediately erodes trust between you and your audience.

Here are three strategies to help you manage your intensity:

1. **Pause when triggered emotionally**
   The most crucial emotional intelligence advice I can offer you is to become a master at *pausing*. Pausing disrupts the hijacking that happens in the amygdala part of your brain, and helps you get back to your higher-level thinking space. Pausing can help ensure your next move is one you don't regret.

2. Name it to tame it

After you pause, immediately identify the emotion you feel. Classifying your feelings can dampen their charge. It allows you a chance to regain control, and express what you feel so you can make better choices on how to move forward. As Dr. Phil said, "You cannot change what you do not acknowledge."

3. Know what your body is saying

More than 65% of how you communicate is nonverbal. Yet most people have no clue about what their body language is saying. Body language is about perception, not what you want it to mean. Your body contains four power zones: neck dimple, torso, naughty bits, and feet.

How you use those power zones will largely determine if you come across as confident and powerful or empathetic and collaborative.

67% of your leadership presence is based on gravitas and your ability to stay calm under pressure. Your intensity has a direct impact on how others perceive your character and leadership ability.

TIP #8:
Play the long game

I had a boss who once told me that if I wanted to lead effectively then I needed to learn how to slow down and take people with me. She said, "Your problem is that you're ten steps ahead of everyone else. You need to slow down and let others buy into the process."

She was right. I was playing a short-term game to the finish line. I was primarily focused on me, laser-focused on what needed to happen to get to the finish line quickest, and dragging everyone else along. I took their lack of speed as a measure of their incompetence, and my ego made me believe it was up to me to save the day! It was exhausting for all of us.

I've known several newly-promoted leaders who wanted to make a quick mark and impress people. They showed up every day ready to shake things up, but they were too aggressive in their approach. Lacking buy-in from the people on their teams, they started to deconstruct and reassemble things. Leaders like that usually don't last very long.

Leadership presence requires you to play the long game, by keeping your eye on the long-term outcomes.

Here are five steps you should take when playing the long game:

1. Remind people of the end goal
2. Check in with the team frequently
3. Hold back when necessary
4. Give others their moment in the spotlight
5. Celebrate together

You can be a master at your game without having to prove it with every move. Sometimes you need to let go of the short-term moment so you can win the long-term game.

TIP #9:
Stop putting your identity on the line

The core of your self-worth is rooted in what and who you believe you are. If you want to change your presence, then you must be willing to change your beliefs about who you think you are.

I used to become defensive whenever someone challenged my perspective, offered constructive or provided unwarranted feedback on my ideas.

I worked so hard to grow myself and my career that I unconsciously identified "who I am" as those things. Therefore, whenever someone spoke to me in a way that challenged those ideas, I took it as them challenging me and my character. As a result, I lashed out or detached.

You cannot authentically connect and build trust when you are waging an internal war and fighting for your identity.

Leadership presence requires you to be aware of your identity triggers and learn to separate yourself from any external form of identity. When we do this, we stop taking ourselves so seriously, and we don't allow others to dictate our emotional wellbeing and self-worth.

TRY THIS EXERCISE!

1. Answer the question, "Who am I?"
2. Do not answer with any title.
3. Start by saying, "I am someone who . . . "
4. Go below the surface to who you really are, what you stand for, why those things are important to you, and where you learned them.

Stay true to this authentic version of yourself. Nothing anyone says will ever be able to bother you once you learn to separate their opinion and truth from who you truly are.

You will immediately improve your relationships and communication skills whenever you stop putting your identity on the line in every conversation.

TIP #**10**:
Protect your online presence

What you post online is a direct reflection of your values and character in the moment. It's up to you to protect your online presence.

Social media makes it easy to act impulsively, post or retweet a comment, and forget about it. We often don't realize how many people see those posts and what perceptions they've formed. Those perceptions are impacting what kind of doors open and close for you throughout your entire life.

Your posts don't just impact you, they also impact the reputation of those who are affiliated with you. I talked with an executive who runs a prestigious national membership organization in the United States. He told me they stopped working with a gentleman because of his comments online. His comments did not represent who they are, and they did not feel comfortable being identified with him.

I've been in performance review meetings where leaders complained about someone's online presence and the negative impact it had on that individual's presence and credibility in the workplace. Inevitably, right or wrong, those perceptions impacted that person's forward movement in the organization.

There are numerous celebrities who sabotaged their careers because of what they posted online. Roseanne Barr's show was cancelled hours after an offensive post. Kathy Griffin has struggled to make a comeback after her post about President Trump. Jamal Shuman, a former football player at Elon College, was indefinitely suspended after posting obscene tweets about not getting enough playing time.

Your credibility is more important than likes on social media. Future employers, employees, and fans are going to scour the internet searching for your name and to see if you are the person they believe you to be. What will they see?

One of my favorite Harvard Business Review articles is *Discover Your Authentic Leadership*. It clearly articulates the idea that authenticity is showing up with the same style and values wherever you go. In fact, the authors say, "Think of your life as a house. Can you knock down the walls between the rooms and be the same person in each of them?" Employers want to work with people who are consistent. They want to know you're not a different person online than you are at work. More importantly, they want to ensure you're not going to put their reputation on the line because you failed to think about yours.

We live in a world where youth have grown up with social media, and their entire lives are well documented. We need to remind them that nothing online is private, ever. What they believe now in their teenage years is not what they will believe when they are in their thirties. This doesn't mean you can't share your beliefs and engage in meaningful conversation online. You should, however, be intentional with what you post and how you respond.

Here are three guiding questions that should always drive your decision-making before your post online:

1. Will this post build my credibility/brand?
2. Is this post truthful and kind?
3. Will this post make my momma proud?

Someone once told me, "Just because you have something to say doesn't mean it needs to be said." Protecting your virtual presence means you might feel passionate about certain topics, but you refrain from posting because it's not going to help you build the brand you've worked so hard to build.

Leadership presence is using your style to earn others' confidence and trust. We must be mindful that we are doing that virtually, just as much as we are face-to-face. You must show superior speaking skills in person as well as online.

Pat Summit said, "You can't pick and choose the days that you feel like being responsible." Leaders always accept accountability. You have the freedom to say what you want, but you also own the rewards and consequences of those actions.

Remember: your digital footprint will serve as your legacy long after you're gone.

TIP #11:
Vent in private, lead in public

You have every right to process and express your feelings. In fact, being able to name and understand your feelings is a healthy sign of emotional intelligence. However, do it in private with people who have earned the right to hear it.

When you decide to air out your unexamined feelings in the public domain, especially with people who have little to no context of who you really are, you're allowing intensity to get in your way. It comes across as professional immaturity.

Maybe you'll feel better after venting or calling others out. It might make for good television or a newspaper headline. You might even intimidate others from speaking up and challenging you, but all of those outcomes cost you trust and credibility. It's a lose-lose scenario.

Leading in public doesn't mean never showing emotion. Instead, it means expressing yourself without being emotional in the process.

One of my coaching clients had a mantra that he would always do his best to respond publicly in a way that his son would be proud of him. If a reaction or response wouldn't make his son proud, then he knew it was better to keep it private.

Leadership presence requires you to be aware of your delivery, and to ensure that delivery builds trust with your audience. You erode trust when people talk more about your delivery than about your message.

10 QUESTIONS TO ASK YOURSELF ON LEADERSHIP PRESENCE

1. Which traits do I admire most in other leaders?

2. What does authentic confidence look like?

3. Which feelings do I want to leave on others?

4. Who am I when I am at my very best?

5. What does my appearance say about me?

6. What mantra can I use as a reminder about how I want to show up?

7. How would people describe me, based on my social media presence?

8. What causes me to show up at my worst? What can I do to work on it?

9. In which specific ways does my presence build trust with others?

10. What does it mean to lead gently?

FINAL
THOUGHTS

The end is just the beginning, and now it's time for you to apply what you've learned. My hope for you is that your life is filled with love, happiness, and relationships which challenge you to become better. May your presence be the light that others so desperately need.

I hope you trust in yourself.

I hope you trust in the incredible power that your presence makes on people every day.

I hope you trust in the possibilities of everything that can happen when you allow yourself to show up at your best. That's the version this world needs. Not in the future, but right now!

Great leaders use their presence to make others feel safe, earn their trust, and inspire them to think differently. This is how they shake up the world, gently. You already have everything you need.

Go shake up the world!

JUSTIN PATTON

BOLD
new you

6 Breakthroughs to Playing Bigger in **Leadership**, **Business**, and **Life**

"Bold New You is a road map on how to lead better and how to just be a great human being. We need more messages like these in business and in leadership."
JOHN FULLER, CEO of THE COFFEE BEAN & TEA LEAF

Order your copy on Amazon today!

BOLD NEW YOU

If you're looking for a leadership book that will help you become a better leader of yourself so you can be a better leader of others, then *Bold New You* is the right choice.

Bold New You empowers you to take an honest look at where you are today, and challenges you to make intentional choices so you can lead and communicate with stronger authenticity.

Bold New You instantly became an Amazon best-selling new release in communication. It won a Bronze Award from the Non-Fiction Authors Association and won in the category of self-help from the 2020 Indie Reader Discover Awards.

UNLEASHING POTENTIAL

confidence

30 Messages in **30** Days to empower you
to be a better, more confident you!

JUSTIN PATTON
Photography by Chad Bock

Order your copy on Amazon today!

UNLEASHING POTENTIAL

Unleashing Potential is a 30-day interactive workbook to help you build stronger self-confidence.

This book is printed in full color with beautiful affirmations and two empowering questions to reflect on and discuss each day.

View yourself differently in 30 days, have a personalized book that you can keep and treasure for a lifetime, and develop the leadership presence you want.

Developing authentic confidence is a journey, and this book is the guide to unleashing the potential already inside you!

Unleashing Potential won a Gold Award from the Non-Fiction Authors Association in 2020.

Made in the USA
Monee, IL
29 July 2020